The Zombie of Suburbia

The Zombie of Suburbia

Will J. Jackson

First published in 2015 by
Martin Firrell Company Limited
26 Red Lion Square, London, WC1R 4AG.

Cover painting by Langham Bailey.

www.willjackson.guru

ISBN 978-0-9931786-0-3

The Zombie of Suburbia is intended as a
general guide to focusing thoughts positively.
It is not a substitute for any professional
medical or psychiatric advice or treatment.
Any actions you may take as a result of reading
The Zombie of Suburbia are your own
responsibility and taken at your own risk. The
author and publisher can assume no
responsibility for any individual's actions
or any effect caused by them.

Praise for the Zombie of Suburbia

'Most of the time we ignore our own amazing potential, settling instead for a life of 'limitation and lack' – personified rather brilliantly by Will J. Jackson as our 'inner suburban zombie'. Our zombie, he says, sabotages us whenever we put our heads above the parapet and dare to dream.

'The Zombie of Suburbia is full of helpful tips and strategies for attracting the life we long for. It is simply and clearly written and illustrated with very human anecdotes from Jackson's own struggle with his inner zombie. And it's a salutary reminder that we really do have a choice about how we live.

'Being a modern guru, Jackson co-opts the smart phone as our ally. He suggests we load inspirational words, uplifting music, affirmations and positive comments about ourselves and others, make FaceTime with our 'abundance buddy', and then access them throughout the day, whenever we feel the pull of our inner zombie dragging us back down.

Good plan, considering, as Jackson says, most of us are wedded to our phones 24/7.

'We must learn to act and think as if we are already A-Listers who have confidence and abundance. By this trick of what Jackson calls 'positive knowing', we can gradually change the DNA of our lives.'

HILARY BOYD
Best-selling author of Thursdays in the Park
www.hilaryboyd.com

Thanks

The author would like to thank the following people for their help and inspiration:

Martin Firrell, Carly Lewisohn, Langham Bailey, Jason Heath, Hilary Boyd, Chris Rickwood, and Rhonda Byrne.

Table of contents

Preface

Preface

In 2008 I believed I was washed up. I was forty-two, in a civil partnership that I was increasingly disillusioned with, and following a career I hated which had made me ill. I was overweight, sad, and felt I had had my one chance at life, and I had blown it. That was the way it was. That was my lot in life. Others had it better. Too bad!

About that time, I had just begun to discover the ideas of New Thought and something called the Law of Attraction. Intrigued by the results that others had described, I began to apply these ideas to my own life, allowing them to become more and more embedded in my day-to-day way of thinking and acting.

Now, it is 2014 and I have a career I love, my perfect partner, my perfect body; I drink champagne at expensive restaurants, walk the red carpet at gala events and hang out with film actors and movie directors.

Want to know how I did it?

This book shares some of the ideas I used to change my way of thinking and change my life from what amounted to a living death into a life of fabulous abundance. All of these ideas can work for you.

Part One

PART ONE:

The zombie, the A-Lister & the smart phone

The power struggle inside you and the tools you have to help the best side win

You might have noticed that there's something going on but you can't quite put your finger on it? It's that feeling you have on 'one of those days' where everything goes wrong. Or that feeling you have when things just seem to fall into place for you, one after the other. Your feelings can be so intense on these occasions, you can almost feel the good or the bad rushing towards you... and that is literally what is happening. Although most people don't realise it, there is a powerful force at work in all our lives. It's the Universal Law of Attraction and it is a natural law governed by our thoughts and actions. This law is enacted by the Universal Mind, and it is through Universal Mind that we are all connected.

Let's have a closer look at what we mean by the Law of Attraction and Universal

Mind. Much has been written about Universal Mind and the Law of Attraction over the years and the principles of these concepts can be summed up in this way. The Law of Attraction is a universal law like the law of gravity. It is working all the time for every one of us and it works on the principle that like attracts like. We are all part of a Universal Mind that connects us to each other and the Universe that we collectively perceive.

Charles F. Haanel writes in his ground-breaking book, The Master Key System: 'The Universal Mind is static, or potential, energy. It simply is. It can manifest only through the individual, and the individual can manifest only through the Universal. They are one.'

Human beings, our thoughts and the Universe we inhabit are made up of energy. If like energy attracts like energy, then positive thoughts attract positive people and circumstances to each and every one of us. We are each an individual thought magnet connected to the whole and we are each creating our own world through our thoughts, whether those thoughts are positive or whether they are negative. Therefore, if we focus on positive thoughts, we attract other people and events that are on that same positive frequency.

Your inner zombie

But there is something holding us back. It's that niggling lack of belief in ourselves and our abilities. It's that disempowering little voice inside that says: 'I can't really have that perfect person. I'm not fabulous enough.' Or: 'Who am I kidding? I can never have that kind of wealth and abundance. I can never earn that much money.' But this is a lie. We need to train ourselves to blank out that little voice inside full of doubt about the true potential of life every time it says: 'Know your place, don't expect the best. Life is hard and full of knocks and you better be careful out there.'

That way of looking at the world is a limited belief system that can prevent us from really living life to our fullest potential. That small-minded view can lead us to believe we can only ever go to a certain level and our lives can only go so far. That kind of negative narrative exists inside many of us and it leads us to the idea that we're just that plain ordinary girl or guy from the suburbs, never destined for greatness. There's nothing special about us – who do we think we are? But everyone is special and amazing and brilliant, and everyone can have an amazing life, no matter who they are or where they are from, if they only learn to tap into the potential of the Universal Law of Attraction, and make it work for them. So we all need to watch out for that small-minded, limited-thinking version of us who prefers that we just exist and get along rather than living the life of our dreams. That side of us is our very own version of the living dead and it wants us to live a life of limitation and lack, shuffling along and merely existing, just as if we were one of the living dead. That version of us is our inner suburban zombie and like any good B-movie zombie, it can pop up at any time to drag us down with those limiting beliefs. Every time it does this, we need to be ready and we need to take our zombie down!

Most of us have been conditioned to think that our lives will be limited and that we have certain parameters within which we must exist: our inner zombie is an expert at this way of thinking. When our zombie is whispering in our ear, the majority of us experience limiting beliefs about the world and the potential in our lives when the truth is we can have absolutely anything we want, be who we want, have the way of earning income we want.

Your inner A-Lister

Fortunately, we all have the ability to defeat our inner zombies. The answer lies in changing the way we think. We have a very powerful tool at our disposal to help us win this battle... and we have a very powerful ally. The tool is our smart phone and the powerful ally is our inner A-Lister. Let's look first at that powerful ally we all have inside. Our inner A-Lister is that version of ourselves who believes in the potential for everything in our lives to be wonderful. Our inner A-Lister has a firm belief that fabulous abundance and happiness is our birthright and that not just good things, but great things, will happen to us. The A-Lister sees the good things that we already have in our lives, no matter how small, and is thankful and joyful about those good things. Our inner A-Lister knows that life has the potential to be absolutely wonderful in every area and you'd better believe they are going to work it so that it is. Our A-Lister wants the best for us and our A-Lister expects to get the best. Our A-Lister sees this as the truth, as inevitable. But you might be asking, if we all have this inner A-Lister inside of us, why are we not all living lives overflowing with untold fabulousness and abundance?

The struggle between your inner zombie and your inner A-Lister

The truth is we are all natural-born A-Listers. As children we display our natural inner A-Lister by dressing up, putting on a show, being centre of attention and expecting the best in the world. But as we grow up we are taught to view this expectation as increasingly unrealistic. We are told that life being fabulous and amazing is a nice idea, a lovely little pipe dream, but in reality it is just not so. As we grow up, we don't use our imagination and play so much. We are told that life happens to us, that we must take what life throws at us and aim to get a good job so we don't starve. Education and adulthood bring the idea of fear, limitation and lack. They bring the idea of what we can't do and the belief that life is full of toil and uncertainty over which we have little or no control. We grow up to learn to embed those feelings of low expectation and disappointment. That sets up the rise of our inner zombie. Our zombie tells us we are to know our place in life and we can only achieve so much.

The damning little voice of our inner zombie comes out when we have doubts about the unlimited potential available to us.

This happens regardless of whether we are woman or man, older or younger, gay or straight, whatever race, culture, identity or any other circumstance. If we allow our zombie to be in control then we are connecting to the negative frequency which must bring negative things into our lives, but if we unlock and channel our inner A-Lister, we are connecting to the positive frequency which, by the same token, must bring the positive into our lives.

Ever since you were born, you have been raised on a diet of limited expectations. And the voice of your inner zombie will pop up at any time to pull the rug from under you whenever you take that running jump at the life of your dreams.

Your inner suburban zombie is on a mission to keep you in your place at every opportunity, so the question is: are you going to let this happen? Or are you going to take your zombie down? After all, who wants to live in a world of downtrodden limitations when life can be such a fun game... if you only know how to play it… if you only know how to unlock the potential of your inner A-Lister and challenge those lies of lack. This book will help you defeat your zombie and put your A-Lister in the driving seat. It will empower you to change your thoughts and reflect those thoughts in your actions. It will provide you with strategies to power up a mighty weapon to aid you - your smart phone. You will learn how to use this wonderful device to help you focus your thoughts and actions to embed that A-Lister positive mind-set and banish your inner zombie forever.

So, hold on tight and prepare to change your thinking and change your life. Get ready to up your abundance quotient… it's going to be quite a ride! The Fabulous Train is leaving the station… are you on or are you off?

Moving in the direction of your goals through thoughts and actions

It is essential to remember that the Law of Attraction is working all the time. We cannot turn it on or off but we can make it work for each of us to bring more positive experiences into our lives. Belief precedes reality and expectation is the mould into which the jelly of reality flows. Our current lives are the result of our beliefs, thoughts and actions. If we want to improve our lives we need to change the way we are thinking. We need to silence our inner zombie and start paying close attention to our fabulous inner A-Lister.

By channelling your A-Lister you can use the power of right thinking and right actions to attract anything into your life from your perfect partner to your perfect way of earning income. You can be anyone you want to be and you can have the life you want to have. But there is another important thing to be aware of. Let's illustrate it by using the analogy of a body builder. Most body builders will tell you that bodybuilding is a game of two halves. Half of the change in muscle growth comes from what you are eating and half from what you are lifting. It is the same with channelling your A-Lister. You have to focus on the fabulous abundance that you want, and expect to receive it. But that is only half of what you need to do. The other half consists of taking action in the direction of travel towards the fabulous abundance you want and expect. Sitting on the sofa expecting to win the lottery isn't the best way forward if you want to become rich – you aren't really moving in the direction of the money are you? You need to get out in the world and do something to bring wealth to you.

This book will help you take action towards your goal, including thinking and acting as if you already have what you want so that the Law of Attraction will bring what you want to you. But this is not a quick fix. It could take a while... so don't lose focus and don't give up hope.

Focusing on what you want, not on what you don't want

Here's an example that really brought home to me the principle of the Law of

Attraction when I saw it in action before my very eyes. A good friend of mine, who lived out in the countryside in Dorset, was coming to stay with me in London. Being used to a less hurried way of life, she talked often about how unbearably fast London was and how she hated the London Underground because she felt it was so crowded with people jostling against one another.

Of course, there is some truth in what my friend was saying. London is one of the fastest moving cities in the world and the London Underground moves millions of people each week. I was a regular user of the underground and had developed a strategy that really worked. I would listen to relaxing music, my favourite hits or an audio book on New Thought and the Law of Attraction whenever I was on the underground. This would have the effect of immersing me in the sounds of my choice and distancing me from that sense of being jostled, hemmed in and squashed up against others. It would quite literally take me out of the situation, emotionally speaking.

Over time, my experience of the underground became that of the A-Lister and therefore quite different from my friend's. I would attract the experience of travelling on the underground without feeling jostled and trapped every time I got on a train. My friend however had a uniformly different experience when she used the underground. She would find herself in train carriages with standing room only and then get stuck in a tunnel. This was something that would happen to me much more rarely even though I travelled on the underground more often. But then this was inevitable when you think about it: no one jostles an A-Lister, do they? No one keeps an A-Lister waiting in a tunnel, or anywhere else. I was getting the best experiences on the underground through the Law of Attraction and my unfortunate friend was getting the worst, through the action of the same law.

On the day my friend came to stay, she spent a long time telling me how she hated the underground. Her inner zombie had done a real number on her as she came to meet me. So she arrived expecting the worst rather than the best. When we got onto the underground train, even though the carriage wasn't particularly full, she seemed agitated and tense. What happened to her next was incredible. People who got on or off the train knocked into her or brushed against her, a man listening to some music backed into her and someone else swung round with a large bag and knocked her legs from under her. As these things happened, she became more irritated, thus attracting more of the same experiences to her. All of this took place in a half empty carriage. Needless to say, no one knocked into me at all. The next day, a similar thing happened again. She was pushed and jostled and left the train carriage with her feathers well and truly ruffled. My experience of the same journey, even though I was next to her the whole time, was the complete opposite.

If you believe something is true and put your energy and emotion into that belief then it will be true... for you. The question is, to what degree do you want your truth to be negative or positive? Are you going to let your zombie dominate your thinking and drag you down into the zomboid slime from whence it came or are you going to have the gracious, wonderful experiences of someone on life's A-List? The power really is in your hands.

The power of positive knowing

Not so long ago, I was talking to a small group of people about my work with the Law of Attraction. I had explained my theory about the inner zombie every one of us harbours, and the fabulous potential of channelling your inner A-Lister instead. As soon as I had finished speaking, one of the people in the group turned to me and said: 'Ah, yes. Its positive thinking isn't it?' When I thought about this later, I felt more and more that this view was a dangerous and misleading simplification of the concept of focusing your thoughts to bring about change.

I realised that what we are talking about here is most definitely not positive thinking – it is positive knowing. There is a big difference between the two. Positive thinking suggests keeping smiling through in the face of adversity, soldiering on through the bad times, as it were.

Positive knowing is that firm and unyielding expectation that underpins everything and brings about true change for the good. Here is an example that illustrated this perfectly for me. When I first moved back down to London after my divorce, I was living at my dad's, knew almost nobody and was saving for a mortgage. My zombie was waiting in the wings to bring me down with those niggling doubts that I was washed up, too old to be attractive and would probably struggle to find a nice property to buy. In fact zombie began to whisper that I would more than likely have to make do with a place I didn't really want but at least it was a roof over my head. Rubbish of course, but our inner zombies have the tendency to rise up most powerfully when times are tough and they see the chance to teach us where we belong and what we should expect. In other words we belong way down there and we should expect very little! But I decided instead to focus on what I really wanted, to beat back my inner zombie, and channel the A-List version of me.

I had started my great new job with UNICEF UK and after waiting a few months to get settled in, I began the search for an apartment. I wrote down exactly what I wanted on a piece of paper and stuck it on the wall opposite my bed.

Two-bedroom apartment, upmarket area of London, top floor, secure entry phone, lovely neighbours, great price, freehold.

This, my A-List me decided, was what I was going to get!

Property prices were in the doldrums so things were looking good price-wise, but as usual those very helpful news reports on the television and radio, with their idea that bad news gets viewers and listeners, were already saying that the property boom was about to start up again and prices would rise sharply. Estate agents also told me point blank that to get a freehold apartment was nigh on impossible. Undeterred, I took my time. I was the confident A-Lister, who believed I would get exactly what I wanted. After viewing one particularly dingy and depressing apartment, my sister remarked on the apartments opposite with their beautiful ornamental gardens and pretty slate roofs.

'I heard that they are supposed to be gorgeous inside,' she breathed.

When I asked the estate agent he told me there were no apartments available in the block and they were about £30,000 out of my price range. Again, undeterred, I carried on my hunt for an apartment, determined to be neither rushed nor in a panic. The area I had decided I wanted to live in was called South Woodford and was on the edge of East London which was about fifteen miles drive from my dad's house in Ongar, Essex. Knowing that the Law of Attraction cannot distinguish between pretending and the real, I knew I had to act as if I had what I wanted already. Therefore I would drive to South Woodford, park up near the block I was interested in and take the train into London for work. I did this even if it was freezing cold or snowing. This added an extra half hour to my journey each day but I was determined to act the part of someone who had a place in South Woodford already. One morning I was walking towards the station, having parked my car in a side street, when a voice in my head said: 'Take a look at the estate agent's window.' I was amazed to see that an apartment in the block my sister had pointed out had just come onto the market. Immediately I felt: 'That's the one!' I knew instinctively that I didn't need to panic or rush. I expected the apartment eventually and inevitably to be mine.

I viewed it with both my sisters and loved it. I took a picture of the block of apartments and saved it as the screensaver on my smart phone. Every time I got my phone out for any reason, I would see the apartment. My phone became a powerful tool, helping me focus on the apartment multiple times throughout the day. The smart phone is a very effective tool in supporting your focused thoughts on whatever you want. We will explore many more wonderful ways you can use your phone to help you throughout this book.

I made an offer for the apartment and... it was rejected. I was disappointed but my A-Lister was undeterred. I now had a focus for my daily travels from Ongar to South Woodford and onto work. Each day I would park up outside my dream apartment, put on my favourite uplifting music on my smart phone headphones and walk from there to the station, PLAYING THE PART of Will J. Jackson who owned that apartment and was happily going to work listening to his favourite uplifting tunes on his phone.

I put in more offers for the apartment and they were again rejected, so I stopped making offers but continued my daily ritual, knowing the apartment would eventually be mine. I photocopied the estate agent's letterhead and retyped each letter declining my offer changing the wording to a congratulatory acceptance letter and stuck it on the wall opposite my bed. I took the property details the estate agent had given me the first time I viewed the apartment and stuck them on the wall with the words THANK YOU written across in bold red ink. I wrote my name on envelopes with the address of the apartment and stuck them on the wall too! I asked a friend who was also interested in working with the Law of Attraction to send me a congratulatory email about having acquired the apartment. I looked at this regularly and it helped me adopt that mind-set of acting as if I already owned the apartment, as if it was already true.

I was pulling out all the stops on this one. Occasionally, my inner zombie moaned and whispered words of doubt: I should give up the ghost as this apartment was out of my price range; who was I kidding if I thought I could ever have it? In response to this zomboid nonsense, I redoubled my efforts and focused even harder on what I wanted, unlocking the potential of the A-List me who gets what he wants effortlessly. This is an important thing to remember. You must expect to get what you want and it should feel fun, easy and effortless. If it feels worrisome and as if you are forcing yourself to believe then you are defeating yourself. The A-Lister wants and expects effortlessly to get; the zombie needs desperately and pins all its hopes on the outcome. Your inner zombie's desperation attracts more needing, not getting. Want it but don't become attached to the outcome, act and think like a true A-Lister, relax, expect, don't be needy. Needy is the way the inner zombie thinks. And that's the way to keep your desire forever just out of your reach.

I had been focusing on getting my dream apartment for several weeks. I drove to the block as usual, parked up, walked to the station and made my way to work when the estate agent called. She said there had been no other interest in the apartment and asked if I was still interested in buying? I said I was and after some negotiation, we agreed a price. I purchased the apartment and got it for exactly the price I wanted. Not only that but the vendors and the estate agent very kindly made a generous donation to UNICEF as well!

And by the way, the apartment was everything that I had wanted when I first wrote my wish list:

It was two bedrooms, top floor, secure entry phone, freehold and had lovely neighbours! All because I knew what I wanted and I played the game of acting as if I had it already. I successfully ignored the moans and groans of my inner zombie. I bludgeoned my zombie into silence by setting off to work each day from outside the apartment I did not yet own as if it were already my own. Like a confident A-Lister, I simply and effortlessly expected to get exactly what I wanted and I did!

The personal mind-set mantra

Anyone can apply the principle of "expecting it to get it". Develop an A-List mind-set, focused on fabulous abundance, and your life will improve. So why not try some of these personal mind-set mantras? Why not type them into the notes section in that brilliant tool your smart phone so you can look at them throughout the day and embed your A-List mind set:

You can think about your future plans or desires, whether they be around wealth, relationships, career or whatever, and say to yourself: 'This fabulous train is leaving the station and I am on it!'

You can look at life this way: 'Life is a spiral: you can talk it up or you can talk it down – and let me tell you, I am most definitely talking it UP!'

Think about your future desires and say 'I'm ready for an upgrade or I'm getting an upgrade!'

Whatever you want, if you genuinely expect it, you will get it. Playing the part of already having it is a powerful way of silencing your inner zombie. Effortless, relaxed expectation is the A-Lister's way of helping the Universal Law of Attraction do its job of bringing to you what you believe to be true. It has to do so. It has no choice. It is quite simply – inevitable.

Part One of The Zombie of Suburbia has laid out for you the big picture. You have discovered how our lives are pulled between two opposing forces – the negative zombie expecting the worst and the positive A-Lister expecting the best. You have learned how the dominating force in our mind-set whether it be the zombie or the A-Lister is attracting to us the good or bad experiences we are having at any one time. The kind of life we each have is determined by the outcome of the power struggle between the living-dead zombie and the effortlessly expecting A-Lister. The tools we have to tip the balance of power are our thoughts, our actions and that powerful pocket gadget the smart phone. You literally hold in your hands the power to unlock the unlimited potential of the A-list you and vanquish your inner zombie.

Part Two is all about confronting your inner zombie as it reveals its true nature as one of the living dead. Just when you think you've defeated it, up it gets again and puts its cold clammy hands around your hopes and dreams, doing its best to drag you down. The good news is there's more than one way to deal with your inner zombie.

PART ONE: Top tips

Understand the power struggle within and help tip the balance in favour of the fabulously abundant A-List you:

i.   The powerful force at work in all our lives is the Universal Law of Attraction, the natural law governed by our thoughts and actions.

ii.   There are two versions of you, the inner zombie and the inner A-Lister.

iii. Our zombie is that part of us that believes in lack and limitation, our A-Lister believes in unlimited potential and fabulous abundance. There is a battle between the two for control of the way we think and all too often our zombie is winning.

iv.   Channelling your zombie attracts the worst situations and experiences in life, but by channelling your A-Lister you will attract the best.

v.   Are you going to let your zombie dominate your thinking and drag you down or are you going to bring about the abundant experiences of someone on life's A-list?

vi.   Think and act "as if" in order to get what you want. A-Listers are confident and effortlessly expect to get what they want without being attached to the outcome. Zombies are needy and full of fear that they won't get what they want. Zombies are achingly attached to the outcome and so work against themselves by attracting more reasons to need the outcome. Therefore, by the Law of Attraction, the outcome they want will be always out of their reach.

vii.   You have a mighty weapon to help you embed the mind-set of the A-List version of you and that weapon is your smart phone.

viii. Use your smart phone to develop a portfolio of words and phrases to help you focus your expectations on fabulous abundance. Look at these often to develop that successful A-List mind-set. After all most of us have our phone on us all day. And even at night when we are sleeping, our phone is probably charging next to our bed! Make your phone work for you. Your phone is a wonderful resource in helping bring to you the things that you desire.

ix. Use the ideas in this book so that your own story of the Zombie, The A-Lister and The Smart Phone is one where the A-Lister wins through to bring you the life of your dreams.

Part Two

PART TWO:
Defeat your zombie
How to take your inner zombie down (again, and again, and again)

Your inner zombie goes shuffling through life, moaning and groaning about everything that's wrong without taking action to put it right. Often you are channelling your zombie without even knowing it because you have been raised, since first memory, on a diet of fear, lack and limited expectations.

If you were, for a moment, to imagine your life as a movie or television show, it is easy to see how the script has been written. In the struggle between the two versions of us, the zombie and the A-Lister, many of us have given the zombie the leading role in the show. It has become all about that zombie way of thinking and living. But if you understand the principles of Universal Mind and the Law of Attraction, you can become the director and scriptwriter of what happens in your life. You can write an increasingly bigger part for the

A-Lister as your life show progresses. You might even write that inner zombie out of the show altogether if you really apply yourself.

When we work with an understanding of the power of Universal Mind and its influence over the Universal Law of Attraction, we realise one thing very quickly: it is not something that brings us changes overnight. It is not something that we can spend a little bit of time on until we get bored and then abandon it. We need to embed this mind-set firmly in our lives if we want to ring the positive developmental changes. We need to regard it as even more than a mind-set, as a way of thinking, a way of being, a way of life. We have to go for it tooth and nail because our greatest enemy is half-heartedness.

Start your day as an A-Lister full of the beans of life, love and laughter. Watch how your day begins to change in small ways. Over time, your entire life will begin to change too. To use the weight training analogy again, you don't lift heavier and heavier weights and think your body will stay looking the same do you? This principle is also true with changing your thoughts and actions. It will begin to make a difference as you attract better situations and people into your life and as you build up those feelings of positive change.

Similarly if you start weight training, you can't just increase the weights you lift and expect to look like Arnold Schwarzenegger by nine o'clock the next morning. It's a process and it takes time. It took from 2008 to 2014 for me to fully transform my life and some things are still a work in progress. This is not a quick fix, but who in their right mind would want to change their lives with a quick fix anyway? The term 'quick fix' implies plastering over the cracks and repairing or remoulding things in a way that has no thoroughness or durability. And just like a bad decorator changing a room, pretty soon the old cracks will be visible in the paintwork again.

Using A-Lister affirmations to bring positive change into your life

A-Lister affirmations can be great preparation for far-reaching and durable changes in your life. They are an invaluable way of changing your mind-set from focusing on lack and limitation to focusing on fabulous abundance. They are the quickest way to silence your inner zombie and favour your inner A-Lister. A very wise woman once told me that as she got out of bed each morning, she would clap her hands and say out loud: 'Today is an amazing day!' You can do any action or say any phrase you like but, if you follow this ritual, it's important to bear in mind that you must believe that the day will be amazing. Don't just pay lip service to the idea because that way nothing will really happen. It is belief that shapes the reality we perceive. For example, when I realised that the job I was doing had the potential to overwhelm me, I identified how I wanted things to be different. I would get out of bed in the morning and say to myself: 'Everyone I meet is kind and helpful to me and I always get my work done in the allotted time.' The more I made these affirmations the more I found that over the course of about a month, I did increasingly engage with helpful and co-operative people at work and less and less did I have to work beyond 5.30pm. Within three months I never worked past 5.30pm. If anyone was difficult, I continued my positive focus by thanking them in my thoughts for teaching me how NOT to behave. If I had given in to anger, I would have energised my inner zombie giving it the power to rise up and moan that 'people are always difficult'. Getting angry would only attract more difficult people into my experience. This non-aggressive, A-List approach meant it was months before even the whiff of a difficult character or situation came my way in my professional role. Be grateful for everything you are learning from situations and from others. Always ask: 'What are they or what is this teaching me about choosing the right thoughts to bring me a more fabulous and abundant life?'

There can be many things that we want to change in our lives and it can be helpful to have more than one A-Lister affirmation on the go at any one time. Using the affirmations throughout the day helps to embed that mind-set change.

Here, again, your smart phone can be a powerful tool. I found it really worked for me to make good use of the voice memo facility on my phone. It took no more than a minute to record my set of affirmations. For example, I chose: 'Everyone I meet is kind and helpful to me; I always get my work done in the allotted time; Fabulousness and abundance flow to me all the time; I am confident and accomplished; Everyone wants to be me!' You can choose any affirmations you like and I would advise that you read the whole set through three times in your recording to help re-enforce them on playback. I would also suggest no more than two or three to start off with so you get used to the idea and embed the affirmations in your mind. Then expand the list later as you become more familiar with the process. In the end you may have a list of twenty or more, all describing the life you want for the A-List fabulous, abundant new you. Listen to your A-Lister affirmation recording on the train, walking down the street, at the gym, walking round the supermarket and so on. Be sure to identify all those in-between times when, instead of day dreaming or thinking about the bad things, you can listen to your A-Lister voice memo on your phone's headset and get right on it! This will defeat your moaning zombie who focuses on things you don't want and help unlock your A-list potential to attract what you do want into your life.

Starting your day the A-List way

I also found it invaluable to place my own personal ban on all that horrible bad news we are bombarded with as soon as the radio comes on in the morning. Instead, I decided to replace it with uplifting music. This worked brilliantly and really set me up to attract a fabulous day filled with great people and positive experiences. I found it was easier to have music without lyrics as it helped me focus on the joy I wanted for the day rather than being influenced by words that were not my own and were not a true reflection of the thoughts I wanted to have in my head.

It is easy to download music that is uplifting and that works for you. I chose music from songs I had heard with tunes that were vibrant, bouncy, light and uplifting. I then downloaded, not the original song with lyrics, but the Karaoke version. Next, I made up a playlist of those tunes on my smart phone and when I got up in the morning, I put the playlist on shuffle, put my earphones in, and danced around the kitchen making my tea and cereal; I felt fabulous even if it was windy, rainy and dark outside. The impact this had on my day was nothing short of what some people might call a miracle. Things would be better throughout the day, from getting a seat on a crowded train, to getting through all my emails at work. Some of the tunes that worked for me were the karaoke versions of The Promise by Girls Aloud, Am I the Same Girl? by Swing out Sister, The Spell by Alphabeat, Firework by Katie Perry and Backtrack by Rebecca Ferguson, but there are plenty of wonderfully uplifting tunes out there and I am sure you are already thinking of the ones you want to download right now. Get right on it and start your day the A-List way!

Learning the lesson when your zombie rises up again

It is important to note, while using these strategies for developing and embedding your new mind-set, that zombies have the disconcerting habit of rising up from the dead.

As in the best horror B-movies, just when we think our heroes have defeated the zombies, those unhelpful undead have a nasty habit of popping back up, ready to cause trouble all over again. I had been working with the Universal Law of Attraction for a while, and bringing more and more sumptuous and wonderful experiences into my life. I had my perfect partner, I was meeting interesting and influential people, I was going to exciting places and events, I had a job I loved and great work-life balance. But I came to learn that I had to be vigilant. My inner zombie could still get in the way and do what it does best... be the devil on my shoulder who said such helpful things as: 'You are way out of your league mixing with these sophisticated people. You are totally out of your depth and it's beginning to show.' Or: 'Don't you get too used to this lovely life young man – it could all end tomorrow! Then where will you be?!!'

One night, I was going out with my partner to dinner and we had arranged for his driver to take us. This was very new to me and admittedly I was thrilled by the experience. I loved sitting in the back of the black Mercedes in the gladdest of my glad rags being driven through central London. Every time we stopped at traffic lights, people passing by would glance in wondering who we were. What a blast!

After about twenty minutes, we arrived at our friends' house in Battersea. Our driver pulled up, got out and opened the door on my partner's side for him to get out of the car. My inner zombie popped up straight away. Surely I couldn't let the poor driver walk all the way round the back of the car and open the door for little old me as well? Who did I think I was? In that moment I became totally unsure of what to do. Should I bolt across the back seat and get out on the other side? Should I open the door on my side of the car myself? Too late! My partner got out, his door shut and driver walked round the back of the car and opened my door. 'Ooh, thank you,' I said sheepishly as I climbed out. When we arrived back at the apartment, later that night, driver pulled up and as before opened my partner's door. Quick as a flash, I scooted across the back seat and exited on the same side as my partner. Our driver looked a little startled. 'I've come out on this side!' I said as if trying to make it clear that my actions had saved him the trouble of having to walk round the back of the car and open the door for me.

As we walked inside I felt no small measure of awkwardness and confusion. In response, my partner told me two important things. Number one - part of the service (and the fee for being driven somewhere in a limo) is for the driver to open the door for you, even if you have to wait for him to walk round to your side of the car to do it. Number two – chauffeurs take pride in their professionalism and on doing a great job, which includes opening the passengers' doors for them… so let him do his job. I was determined that next time I was driven anywhere, my inner zombie wasn't going to get a look in! There was only room for two in the back of that limo and zombie wasn't coming along for the ride!

Most of us can find examples where our inner zombie has whispered negative assertions in our ears, making us feel uncomfortable, not good enough, not deserving of success or VIP treatment. Zombie has made a career of that relentless who-do-you-think-you-are?! undermining attitude. So when zombie gets the better of you (and zombie gets the better of all of us at some time or another) don't beat yourself up about it. Just take it as a lesson learned and aim to channel your A-Lister next time. In future, be ready to fight back with an A-List affirmation: 'I am more than good enough and can expect to enjoy the best of everything!'

Sometimes, in social situations, we can feel like a fish out of water. Zombie loves that. We think we're not worthy of attention or interest: 'Oh, it's only little me! I'm not good enough to be here! I'm not clever enough! I'm not stylish enough!' There zombie stands with arms folded, shoulders hunched and that voice that says: 'Oh, don't let them go to any trouble. You don't want to put anybody out.' If you think you are not worthy of gold star service, if you think you are not high enough up the pecking order to feel comfortable in a high society situation, then this will become true for you. By the Universal Law of

Attraction, you will encounter situations where you are made to feel not worthy or you will find yourself on the receiving end of the exact opposite of gold star service, no matter how much money you have actually paid.

Inner zombie is trouble with a capital T and you have got to take that zombie down! That zombie has definitely got to go! But beware... even if you think you've seen your zombie off once and for all... it has those zombie qualities of being able to pop up again when you least expect it to. So you need to keep ever vigilant. It's time to make a vow and to say: 'Old me - RIP. New me - VIP.' You are as important and worthwhile as anyone else in any situation so don't you forget it!

Here's another example of how, shortly after I thought I had got rid of my inner zombie for good, it popped up in my life once again. I had just started developing my ideas for helping others to know, understand and use the principles of New Thought when a friend suggested to someone over dinner that

I could coach him on changing his thinking to bring abundance into different areas of his life. I had been studying a coaching course at the time and was half way through it. Now our inner zombies are strong believers that you can't get on in a new career if you don't have a qualification for it. Zombie will tell you: 'You need that certificate in your hand – it's what people expect!' In truth, I was already vastly qualified with my background in advisory work, holistic therapy and developing approaches with young people to improve their well-being. However, did I take any notice of those facts? No, I didn't! My inner suburban zombie won through. I turned sheepishly to my friend and said: 'Oh, I can't coach him yet… I'm only on unit five of my course!!' Down went my self-esteem and aspirations in one single sentence. So watch out! No matter how often you thwart that inner zombie, as in the best horror movie franchises, up it pops again. So stay vigilant! Keep an eye out for your zombie and don't let it get the better of you in the sequel!

Doing the zombie dance

It is easy to understand the concept of focusing our thoughts and actions in order to bring change into our lives. But in the day-to-day challenges of life, it can be just as easy to lose our way. We realise half way through the day that we have been allowing our zombie to be in control the majority of the time. We have been focusing our thoughts far too much on what we don't want. All too easily we can lose heart and lose momentum. This is when it is essential to take your zombie down instantly. Here's how I found a really great way to do just that. I was having a very challenging time at work. The pressure was really on. I found my mind wandering into dangerous territory focusing on how bad everything was. As I was shaving, getting ready for work one morning, my head was full of problems that seemed insurmountable – performance targets that could never be achieved, my pressurised boss venting his frustrations on me and others. I felt trapped in an unbreakable cycle. As yet another whiny depressing thought swirled in

64

my mind, I stopped myself suddenly. I realised how ridiculous my constant negative focus was. I realised my inner zombie was in total control.

I put my razor down. I stuck my arms out in front of me. I rolled my eyes. I groaned and moaned like the best horror movie zombie on the cinema screen. This ludicrous zombie dance worked a treat. As I made fun of my zombie, my mood lifted. I exposed my negative mind-set for what it really was. Within seconds my negative thoughts began to evaporate. I began to see instead the wonderful things around me that I was grateful for. I straightened up and channelled my A-Lister. I noticed how sunny it was outside, I noticed the steaming coffee cup that contained my delicious morning coffee and I remembered I was meeting up with a dear friend after work that evening. I was back on the A-List of life and it felt great.

Within ten minutes of course my zombie rose up again. I started to think about my work frustrations again. So I did my zombie dance again. By ridiculing my inner zombie I undermined its hold over me and had fun in the process. Throughout the day I would continue to do this, making sure I found a quiet place to do my zombie dance. If that wasn't possible I simply pictured myself doing the outlandish zombie dance. This had a similar uplifting effect. As the day progressed, my mind-set became more positive and brought more positive experiences to me. By the end of the day, my overworked and stressed boss had even sent me three very complimentary emails!

Over time, this zombie dance has enabled me to close down thoughts of what I don't want. So next time your zombie takes control, take away its power by ridiculing its woe-is-me worldview. Invent your own wacky zombie dance! Ridicule your inner zombie to put it back in its box. Then stop and notice all the good things around you that put you on the A-List of life.

Everyone has experienced the kind of zombie attack that happens in the small hours of the morning. We lie in the dark unable to sleep because of concerns about finances, work, relationships or whatever else is worrying us. This is the perfect time to bring out your zombie dance. Move your limbs gently as if you were a groaning, moaning, wailing zombie. It may feel quite strange. But this zombie dance will banish those dark and doom laden night-time worries. As you ape your inner zombie in this humorous way you rob it of its power. Your negative thoughts begin to subside. It becomes easier to focus instead on the good things in your life. Cast your mind towards the coming sunrise when your zombie will have shuffled off, defeated, into the far horizon.

Worrying and obsessing about a situation is not improving the situation. It is not helping things and it is not helping you. Take your zombie down using ridicule and you stop it dead in its tracks. You can then approach the situation from a position of strength.

Boosting your A-List potential with some inspirational wallpaper

When I first began working on these ideas of focusing on my A-list wants and listening less to my zombie thoughts of lack, I discovered that if you google a word or phrase, and choose images, often graphic designs of that word or phrase will appear. I tried out lots of phrases and downloaded the images into a file on my phone.

In the end I had quite a collection. I put them into a folder that I titled 'Inspirational' and pretty soon I had well over a hundred words and phrases including: 'Joy', 'Success', 'Today is a great day', 'You are fantastic'; 'Damn you, gorgeous'; 'You are perfect'; 'You are stunning' and so on. I then opened the folder on my phone each morning and randomly chose a positive statement for the day. I then made that statement my smart phone's wallpaper. So now, every time I got my phone out to check an email or text a friend or pretend to be occupied while waiting for someone, my phone said: 'Abundance' or

'Success' or 'Damn you, gorgeous,' or 'You are a genius' or 'You are so fantastic.' Don't underestimate how doing this can begin to embed that positive self-image in your own personal mind-set. It is incredibly easy and fun to set this up in your phone's photo album and it works a treat!

As you begin to see yourself in a more positive A-List light and really believe and feel it, the Universal Law of Attraction will bring more people and circumstances to you to support this belief that you are indeed on life's A-list. It has no choice. When I was newly divorced, living at my Dad's and beginning to dip my toe in the water of the London social scene, I joined a gay men's dining club. I always felt nervous going to meet new people I didn't know, particularly if there was the potential for a romantic connection. I was going to my first session and I had dutifully made 'Damn you, gorgeous' my screensaver. I had looked at it several times on my way to the restaurant where the group was meeting and it felt funny but fun to have this on my smart phone. Every time I looked at it, I thought to myself: 'Men adore me and they fall at my feet.' My inner zombie tried to pop up with its limiting belief telling me: 'Who do you think you are? No-one is looking at you, not with all the gorgeous guys that will be there.' But I took my zombie down and repeated my affirmation: 'Men adore me and fall at my feet' while remembering to look at my phone which displayed the words loud and clear: 'Damn you, gorgeous!'

With this A-List mind-set, I went into the restaurant and stood with the other guys in the group, drinking and chatting before dinner. What happened that night had never happened to me before. Not one, but two men spent the night jostling with each other for my attention, falling over themselves to pay me compliments on how gorgeous they felt I was. They were both very cute guys and by the time we had parted that night I had agreed to meet up with each of them again!

Damn you, gorgeous!

Defeating the army of zombies out there

So far, we have focused our attention on the zombie inside you. We've noted its tendency to rise up just when you think it's died for the final time. We've shared the need for constant vigilance. Now we need to acknowledge that it's not just you, it's not just one zombie, because everyone has an inner zombie. You need to be wary of you own, but you also need to be wary of all the zombies inside all the people you encounter in your life. You need the tools to hold off an entire army of everyone else's zombies too!

When you encounter someone whose zombie is in control, they will be easy to spot. They will be negative and critical of things, focusing almost exclusively on how bad things are. When confronted by someone like this, the phrase 'That says more about you than it does about me' is a wise one. People can be under the influence of their zombie (and its unceasing negativity in every area of their lives) without even realising it. They talk about the bad stuff the majority of the time.

Partly this comes from peer pressure: that 'Haven't we all got it bad' attitude that fuels the inner zombie in all of us. So many of us try to comply and join in with: 'Oh my God, how awful for you and look at this situation in my life that is awful for me too!' It's as if we allow ourselves to be swayed by our own inner zombies so as not to be excluded from the group. We give in all too often to the pressure to be part of the group – to be zombies together - and 'complain along'! The wonderful English actress Fenella Fielding once said: 'People are very free with their bad advice!' What an insightful observation. And people are very free with their negative opinions as well. Always remember that the negative things people say are not the truth and they have no power over you... unless you give them power. Your inner zombie will side with the other zombies; your inner A-Lister will side with fabulous abundance - who do you want in charge?

Because other people allow their inner zombies to be in control so much of the time, you are effectively surrounded by an army of zombies, all hammering, groaning and moaning at your door. People whose zombies have taken control will bombard you with their negative view of the world. By the Law of Attraction they are bringing untold negative situations into their lives. Don't get into their sinking ship with them. It's taking on water, it's listing heavily and it's going deeper and deeper down into an ocean of bad. Of course, it's important to remember these people aren't doing this deliberately to be unkind to you. They are letting their inner zombie dominate their thinking and so they have no choice but to focus on what's bad rather than what's good, on what's going wrong rather than what's going right.

Some people may attempt to get you to buy into their negative view of the world in a misguided attempt to protect you from, or prepare you for, what they believe to be life's inevitable disappointments, according to their inner zombies. They believe they are doing you a kindness by helping you to 'toughen up'. Remember Fenella's words: 'People are very free with their bad advice.' What you really need to toughen up to is the onslaught of negativity. It's that which you need to be prepared for and guard against. Now if you are a Star Trek fan, this will be easy! Whenever someone says something negative like 'It's so hard to get a promotion there's so much competition' or 'Works emails are bullies they swamp us don't they?' All you need to do is say to yourself: 'RAISE SHIELDS!' This allows you to become consciously aware of the negativity in the room and then you can guard against taking it on board. Alternatively, if you are of non-Trekker stock, you can use any quick and memorable phrase that works for you. The important thing is that you need to have a phrase to trigger your conscious awareness of negativity so you can defend yourself against it and take its power away.

You might say: 'Close flood gates!' Or: 'Stop right there with that!' Or even: 'Zombie, be gone!' Play around with this until you find the perfect negativity blocker that works for you and then make good use of it. You have to belittle the negativity of others in order to protect your own well-being. And remember, the naysayers are not doing it on purpose. It's only learned negative behaviour, but they are doing it all the same and you need to have your defences in place.

It's not just about you, the Law of Attraction is working for everybody all the time

People can be surly with us for all sorts of reasons (like having had an argument at home that morning or feeling pressured and unhappy at work). None of these reasons has anything to do with us, but how many times do we fall into the trap of thinking that the surliness is all about us. This is because like everyone else, most of the time we are thinking about ourselves. So we think: 'How can that person's bad mood possibly be anything other than something to do with me?' Wrong! That waiter, co-worker, relative, retail assistant can be grumpy for a myriad of reasons. Whatever unhappy face they are wearing that day, nine times out of ten, it's not about you! Don't buy into their bad feelings. Don't bite into their poisoned apple or you risk poisoning yourself and others along with you. Your inner A-Lister only eats the most delicious foods and certainly nothing that is going to make them feel anything other than fabulous!

And anyway, even if somebody were being deliberately unpleasant, the Universal Law of Attraction dictates that their surliness and negativity towards you will undoubtedly bring some strong negativity back into their own personal experience. You may not be there to see it happen, but be assured, happen it most definitely will. After all, it can't fail to happen, can it, if the Law of Attraction is working non-stop in the lives of every single one of us? Think about it. It's inevitable.

Here's how I applied this idea directly in my own life. One New Year's Eve, the person who lived in the apartment on the floor below me and my partner had a party with a DJ and full sound system. It was so incredibly loud that the floor in our apartment was vibrating. This person already had a noise abatement order against them, because of previous loud parties, but didn't seem to care. Now, it was New Year's Eve so we didn't rush to complain but the party did go on until 6am in the morning. By then, we had had enough! We did call the local noise control team but by the time they arrived, the music had finally been turned off so nothing could be done. We had lost an entire evening's sleep and felt groggy and exhausted all New Year's Day.

We could have easily spent the whole of New Year's Day biting into that poisoned apple of anger, frustration and resentment. But we knew that the Law of Attraction was working for everybody, including the person who had thrown the incredibly noisy party that lasted all night long. We therefore held firm in our belief that that person would, at some time in the not too distant future, find themselves on the receiving end of some similarly negative experiences at the hands of others. We knew for certain it would happen even if we didn't ever see it or ever hear about it. The scales of the Universe would ping that person's inconsiderate actions right back to them in some way, shape or form. Less than one month later my partner and I were getting into the lift at our apartment building and we came across the person who had thrown the all-night party. At the tender age of 21, dressed in the latest expensive fashion and living in a luxury apartment in the centre of London, you would have thought this person would be the perfect picture of someone living the life of wealthy, happy abundance, literally full of the joys of spring!

Not so on that day! For some reason, this young person was clearly fed up and scowling. It was definitely the face of someone who had really not had the best of days! It's important not to take pleasure in seeing someone else's misfortune; simply recognise that the Universal Law of Attraction is indeed an irrefutable natural law and it is working for everyone all the time, non-stop.

Getting the best out of other people and your interactions with them

The Law of Attraction works for all people in all situations, including your most personal relationships. If your partner is difficult or negative, you can't force them to change. The only person who can make that change happen is themselves. Internal changes come because people make that internal decision to change.

You cannot change another person for the very obvious reason that you are not them. But you can change how you, yourself think, feel and behave in relation to that person. You may want to look at a relationship or friendship in terms of whether it is working for you.

You can choose to appreciate, and focus on, the positive aspects of the relationship or friendship. Now, once again, your mobile phone is a wonderful tool to help you do this. You can put a picture of the person on your phone and look at it at different times throughout the day. When you do, only ever think of one thing that you like about that person. Then next time you look at the picture, think of something else, or think even harder of the same thing, you like about that person. You can also make use of your notes list on your phone. You can make a list of some of the things you like about the person. In the morning, noon and evening, look at the list on your phone and remind yourself of the things you like about that person.

Although this will not be changing the person inwardly, this process will mean that each time you connect with the person in real life, you will see more and more of the qualities you like about them instead of the ones that you don't want. It will bring more of their good traits into your realm of experience when you are with them. Their negative traits will still be there of course until such time as the person chooses to change, but the difference is that other people will be on the receiving end of those negative traits and not you. Other people will be the ones in the wrong place at the wrong time and on the wrong side of your friend or partner!

I can share with you a direct experience of how this method worked for me in one of my jobs. One of my bosses, a very senior and important person at the office was notoriously difficult. He literally terrorised members of staff, including some of my colleagues with whom I worked very closely. He would bully them to such an extent that even a senior member of staff was reduced to tears. Another colleague began to tremble physically whenever this person came near her. This was a decidedly unnerving situation but I did not let my zombie take control. I chose to focus on my boss's good traits. I reminded myself that although what I was hearing from colleagues suggested that he was a bully, I knew that he appreciated efficiency, and felt passionately about safeguarding all our jobs. He had also brought coherence and clarity of purpose to the project we were working on where previously there had been confusion and an overwhelming lack of direction. I reminded myself how grateful I was for that and I told myself that I only ever had good experiences with him. I made a list of these thoughts on my phone. Consequently in all my years of working with him, I never had one bad experience and I was the only person in my team who was ever able to say this.

Whenever my colleagues related stories about the latest dreadful humiliation they had received at his hands, I listened and supportively agreed that it all sounded dreadful, but I didn't join in the gossip-mongering and criticism – I didn't sign up to that contract binding me to a world of negative experience!

Instead I simply said: 'I haven't found him to be like that with me. It hasn't been my experience of him.' I then re-iterated in my head those good points about him that I had listed on my phone. I felt grateful for them and grateful also that he was courteous and encouraging to me. We often hear parents, carers and teachers tell children: 'If you can't say anything nice about someone else, then say nothing at all.' This may sound like a gooey statement designed to make children behave, but it is actually applying a very important principle of the Universal Law of Attraction. If you focus on the negative in others, then you will get more of the negative in return because that is precisely what you are asking for.

If we encounter a difficult person, it can be very easy to react to them and let their negative nature incite us to rash actions. By doing that, we give our power away to others. In effect, we hand over control to them when we lose control of ourselves. But in truth, each of us shapes our lives by our own thoughts, words and actions. It is important to remember that to blame others, to become angry and react to the negative comments and actions of others, is denying the truth that we hold all the cards, and we have all the power. When we apply ourselves to defeating our negative zombie and unlocking our A-Lister, we make the Universal Law of Attraction work for, rather than against, us. We put our power to the best use possible – filling our lives with fabulous abundance.

Gossip and judging others are never the A-List way

People dominated by their inner zombies will often focus on limitation and lack through the medium of gossip. It is very easy to board the Gossip Train and join in all of that poisonous negativity. We fall into the trap of conforming and becoming part of the zombie group. To defend against this, approach life like a dedicated lawyer and only ever make judgements based on the HARD EVIDENCE!

Here's an example. I wanted to meet up with a relatively new friend who was due to visit London on a business trip in the spring. I really enjoyed spending time with them and they had mentioned a while back how good it would be to meet up. As the time drew near, I emailed them to ask when they would be coming. NO REPLY. Very quickly, my zombie stuck its hands out of the earth, hauled itself up and began mumbling thoughts of doubt and disaster. I waited and waited. I grew quite agitated and started to think that my new friend was ignoring me. Had I done something wrong? What was the reason for their wall of silence? Sound familiar?

Then, about three weeks later, they emailed with the exact dates they would be visiting London and said how much they were looking forward to catching up. I realised the only reason they had not emailed me earlier was because they didn't have the actual dates confirmed, and so they had nothing concrete to tell me! It is very easy, in our technological age, to assume that everyone takes the same approach to text or email as we do. Some people just will not respond unless they have something useful to say; others will be very laissez-faire at responding to any message, and others will ping back to you instantly. None of these approaches is wrong, they're just different. It is important to acknowledge that people approach communication in lots of different ways and it can be helpful not to fall into the trap of being judge and jury before you have the concrete evidence you need to make a proper judgement.

So remember, you can't change other people but you do have the power to bring the best side of them into your experience. Don't join in and focus on the negatives in someone, don't immediately jump into the role of judge and jury. Don't let your inner zombie tell you how you have no control over the situations you attract. Employ strategies that enable you to think about the positives in each person and the Law of Attraction will bring those positive qualities more and more into your realm of experience.

This chapter has explored ways to confront and vanquish the zombie within you and to stand firm against the zombies in others. There is an army of moaning, shuffling zombies out there waiting to infect you with ideas of limitation and lack.

You need to be ready for them, and you need to be vigilant, because like all zombies they can pop up when you least expect them to! Channel the positive thinking, gracious and fabulous A-List you and take those zombies down!

PART TWO: Top tips

How to take your inner zombie down!

i.   Many of us have given our zombie control of the script of our life show as well as the leading role. But the truth is you are the director and scriptwriter of what happens in your life, so you can increase the role of the A-List you as your life show progresses.

ii. You need to invest the time and effort to ring the positive changes in your life. This is not a quick fix. Develop the A-List mind-set and you will get the life you want... over time.

iii. Use A-Lister affirmations to change your mind-set and attract fabulous abundance in all areas. Your voice memo recording app on your smart phone can really help you do this.

iv. Difficult people and situations are helping you to choose the right thoughts to attract fabulous abundance.

v. Ban the news in the morning and download versions of your favourite uplifting tunes to start your day the A-List way.

vi. Protect yourself from others in the clutches of their own zombies and raise your shields against their negative ideas of limitation and lack.

vii. The Law of Attraction is working for each and every one of us, so if someone is inconsiderate or unpleasant then the negativity they put out will return to them in equal measure. So, why would you allow what they have done to upset you?

viii. You cannot make other people change but you can put your attention on the good things about a person. Use your phone to list their good points or put their picture on your phone and think of good things every time you look at it. You will get more of the good you want from that person as a result.

ix.   We tell children: 'If you can't say something nice about someone, don't say anything at all.' In terms of the Law of Attraction, this is superb advice for adults too.

x.   Our inner zombie wants us to assume the worst in any given situation and particularly when evaluating the actions of others. A-Listers have great lawyers and great lawyers base their arguments on hard evidence. Apply this rule in your own life and never judge others on hearsay or gossip.

Part Three

PART THREE:

New you VIP

How to nurture and become the new A-list you

If you have begun to apply the ideas already suggested in this book, then you will be finding that your inner zombie is beginning to lose its power over you. But you must remember to remain vigilant because that zombie version of you, with all its limiting beliefs, has that nasty habit of taking over again just when you really don't want it to. The best thing you can do in these instances is to take it as a lesson learned and redouble your efforts to destroy your zombie again and invoke the A-Lister inside you.

Channelling your inner A-Lister is not about being arrogant, difficult or looking down on others, nor is it about being stunningly good looking; A-Listers come in all sorts of wonderful shapes and sizes, as does beauty itself. Developing the A-List you is about lifting yourself up to a level where you are attracting the best to you. You attract the best when you are feeling worthy of the best. And why shouldn't you? You are fantastic. Yes, THAT MEANS YOU – YOU ARE FANTASTIC! So believe it! This chapter will explore ways to help you to unleash the A-List version of you and unlock those pathways to fabulousness and abundance in every area of your life.

One thing you can do to really help ring the fabulous changes in your life is to get yourself a Fabulous Abundance Buddy. This is very powerful and can boost your rating on life's Fab-o-meter hugely. As you start to use the Universal Law of Attraction to bring great people and situations into your life, you will begin to discover that you are not alone. You will begin to find that more and more people will appear in your life who know about the Universal Law of Attraction and the power of Universal Mind. You will begin to have conversations with others who can share with you how this approach to life has also made a difference to them. If one of these people is a family member, a friend or someone else close to you, suggest that you help boost each other's A List potential by scheduling regular check-ins.

I have been doing this for a while now. Every week I enjoy a one-hour check-in with my buddy. We talk to each other about successes and challenges in getting the most out of the Universal Law of Attraction that week, and we help each other with suggestions and encouragement. If you can't meet face-to-face then you can phone, FaceTime or Skype at an agreed time or check-in via email. These are all things you can do in any quiet place using your smart phone! Bouncing ideas off a like-minded individual is fun and it really works. You can support and inspire each other. You will be able to learn from each other's experiences, avoid making similar mistakes, and bring about those changes you want. You will also be able to explore together the reasons for any setbacks. You can make suggestions to each other about focusing your thoughts and feelings in the most advantageous way to face any upcoming life challenges.

Acting like an A-Lister

Speaking of challenges, one thing our inner zombie will do to pull the rug from under us is to encourage us to change our expectations in line with those of other people. It will moan and groan about knowing your place and not putting anyone out... it will do this in any situation, even one where we might be paying for a service. Here's an example. You go into a restaurant and you really want to have the linguine but you notice it is served with crab. You really hate crab but see baked salmon elsewhere on the menu. Now, you think to yourself, salmon linguine would be great. It's just what you fancy! Your inner suburban zombie, however, couldn't possibly let you put anybody out so you order something else instead of the linguine. Your inner A-Lister would order the linguine but say that she would prefer it with salmon. The question is – what would you do? Are you zomboid and self-defeating or are you gracious and worth it?! Why not power order if you need to and defeat that B movie zombie once more? It's really no hardship for the restaurant to put salmon in your linguine instead of crab.

If we act the part of the A-Lister, the kind of service an A-Lister expects will be reflected increasingly in our experiences. Again, this is not about lording it over others and looking down on people. We will only ever get graciousness and kindness back by giving it out. This is the Universal Law of Attraction reflecting back to us what we put out there. So our A-Lister is always gracious.

If we change the way we think, we begin to change our entire life experiences. Approach life from the mind-set of the disenfranchised shuffling zombie and you will attract more awkward and uncomfortable situations. Do you want to be the apologist handwringer saying sorry for taking up space in the room, or do you want to be the accomplished fantastic version of yourself playing the wonderful game of life? The Universe knows you are worth it... do you?

Accepting a compliment the A-List way

As we focus on being an A-Lister in life, we will attract to us positive people and circumstances. Receiving the gift of a compliment is a good example of this. Sadly, it's not in many people's natures to accept compliments easily, particularly if they are British. We think we are being a nicer person by being self-deprecating, but that is a grave error if we believe in the power of the Universal Law of Attraction. Compliments are a lovely gift. They power up the engine to propel us forward towards a fabulous life. And it is very ungracious to refuse a gift. So when someone gives you a compliment, take it with a firm sense of 'Yes I am!' rather than a sheepish 'Oh what, who me, no surely not!' Unfortunately it is all too easy to do the latter than the former. Here's an example - not so long ago, I was with my partner at a restaurant and the young woman on the desk had the most amazing silky shoulder-length hair. My partner remarked on how fantastic her hair looked. To which she replied: 'Oh, is it? It's very straggly today...!' If you refuse a compliment you are refusing a gift and the giver will not be inclined to offer another one so readily next time.

Accepting the gift of a compliment doesn't mean you have to shout out that you are indeed wonderful in response to every single positive word said about you. That 'Yes I am!' can be something you say inwardly to yourself immediately the person gives the compliment. At the same time, you can channel your inner gracious A-Lister and smile back at them with a warm 'Thank you.' Then return the compliment. It's good to give gifts as well as receive them.

I failed miserably at this when out with some friends once. One of them was talking about a time when I had cooked and prepared a buffet.

'Will made a delicious buffet at his party and he made it all seem so effortless!'

'Oh, no,' I sheepishly responded. 'I just opened some packets of quiche and threw some pasta in a bowl!' In actual fact, I had cooked some things for the buffet as well as heating up some shop bought products, and I had done it without a bead of sweat breaking out on my brow! But my suburban zombie popped up and said: 'That person can't be talking about you, can they? I mean you're hardly Nigella Lawson are you!!??'

Fortunately, as soon as I had responded negatively to the compliment about my organisational skills in the cookery department, I realised my mistake. And realising is a step in the right direction. Now I have learned to accept even the most outrageous compliments wherever I go. And because I love them and am grateful for them, more come flooding in! I have accepted them into my realm of consciousness, into the little bit of space I occupy in the Universal Mind.

There is another very important point to make here - accepting compliments makes them true for us. So if someone says you are intelligent and good at giving advice, saying no to that compliment means you are saying no to being intelligent and good at giving advice. If you say yes to the compliment you will become more and more intelligent and good at giving advice by the Universal Law of Attraction. Similarly if someone says you are good looking, then saying no to that compliment means you don't want it and so Universal Mind will connect you with more and more people who find everyone else attractive... and not you! By accepting the gift of being told you are attractive, you will bring more people into your life who will find you attractive.

Any gift is an act of kindness and compliments are some of the greatest gifts we can give. You shouldn't throw that gift back in the face of the giver. They have taken the trouble to give you the gift so it is ungracious and unkind to them. But it is also just as unkind to yourself. What you are actually doing is declaring: 'I'm not good enough! I don't deserve the gift of that compliment!' It is far better for all concerned if you accept the compliment and say to yourself: 'YES I AM! Yes, yes, yes!!'

Boosting your confidence with the help of your smart phone

One thing I found that worked very well for me was to record the positive things that others said about me on my phone. This is easy to do and can provide a massive boost in the self-image department. All you have to do is set up a new page in your phone's notes pages and call it: 'How others see me.'

Every time I received a positive comment such as 'You always take a great picture' or 'You are so kind and so clever' I would make a note of it in my 'How others see me' page. Next to the comment, I would put the name of the person who said it or was quoted as saying it. So, for example, if Janet Thompson said that I had the most fantastic blue eyes, I would put in my phone: 'You have the most fantastic blue eyes,' - Janet Thompson on Will Jackson. Every so often I would look at those positive and uplifting descriptions of me, and my day would immediately start to travel in the right direction, attracting more positive people and circumstances, upping the level on my own personal Fab-o-meter!

This method can also be useful in a more general sense. It can help us to change our overall way of thinking about our self-image by reminding us of all the good things others have said about us over a period of time. After all, how often do we forget the compliments others give us almost immediately? And once we've forgotten them, how can we possibly embed them in our self-belief system? On the other hand, if someone says something negative we take it on and let it embed in our consciousness. It eats away at us, day in and day out, giving ammunition to our inner suburban zombie when it pops up saying: 'Be more successful? Get your perfect partner? Who do you think you are?' Now you can respond to your zombie with an affirmative: 'I am the one who is loved and admired by others. That's who I am!' And by the Law of Attraction, if you put your energy and emotion into believing this to be true, it will become increasingly embedded in your life experience and will become the reality of your life.

When you are making a decision or exploring a situation in your life, check to see where the decision is coming from. Is it based on fear or does it come from a worldview informed by an understanding of limitless abundance. For example, if you wanted to change your wardrobe and wanted to be a little more flamboyant in your choices, do you immediately start to think about all the ways other people will negatively critique your new look? Or do you think they will be thrilled by your boldness and find you more interesting as a result? The first mind-set is based in fear, the second in limitless opportunity. This is something I can talk about from direct personal experience. Not so long ago, I decided to start wearing hats when I had never worn them before; even the thought of a beanie hat in the winter - a practical piece of apparel for the season - filled me with embarrassment at the possibility of people 'looking at me funny'! My partner had remarked that wearing hats gets you noticed and as we had started going to a lot of art openings together, it seemed like a good idea to try some hats out for size, so to speak. As a very shy person, this was a big and quite scary step for me. I would often need to partake of a little nerve-steadying tipple before stepping out into the night sporting my chosen headgear. As time progressed, I decided to wear hats outside the realms of the 'arty party' and donned a trilby to go for drinks with some friends.

When I got to the bar and met my friends, I was rather anxious about what comments I might get. There were six other people there in total. Two thought I looked great and wanted to try my hat on, four said nothing (but it's important to remember they said nothing negative, perhaps they were in awe of the new exciting hat-wearing me – I choose to think so!). After about an hour, one of them finally said to me: 'So, what's with the hat?' After a full hour of compliments about my hat, up jumped that mean old inner suburban zombie of mine! 'What on earth do you think you're doing? You're just little old you, not Lady Gaga you know!' Channelling all this, I turned to my friend and said: 'Oh, the hat thing? I just thought I'd do something mad today...!' Immediately I had fallen into the trap of basing my statement in fear and lack rather than fun, abundance and strength! What I should have done was channel my inner A-Lister saying: 'I've discovered I absolutely love hats. I've developed a craving for them. I want to wear them more and more. In fact I feel like I want to have a hat on 24/7! Even in bed!'

Make a vow, now, to base your decisions on the firm belief that you have a fantastic future, and make fewer and fewer decisions based in fear. The Universal Mind will bring you more fantastic fear-free experiences when you do.

Marking yourself up, not down

At a party one night, there is a man who we'll call Mr Read. He is widely read, cultured and intelligent and he is chatting with another man who has been introduced to him by a mutual friend. Let's call this person Mr Big. Now, Mr Big knows by reputation that Mr Read is clever and widely read. During the course of the conversation, Mr Big constantly makes reference to things he himself has read. Mr Big asks Mr Read if he has read this particular novel or if he knows that particular play? Of course, if you think about the huge amount of literature that has been written, it's virtually impossible for two people to have read exactly the same novels or plays. It would have been extremely unlikely that Mr Read, however well-read, would have read the same books as Mr Big.

After the conversation ends, Mr Read feels like he has been utterly put through the grinder by Mr Big in what seemed like a malicious game of conversational one-upmanship. But if you flip that way of thinking on its head, you could perhaps encourage Mr Read to look at the situation in a totally new light. Was it really a case of one-upmanship or was Mr Big so in awe of Mr Read's intelligence that he was simply trying to keep up? Quite often in these kinds of situations we can be like Mr Read and assume that other people are putting us down when actually they are trying to cover up their own sense of inadequacy. Not so BIG now, are they...? Think about this story again. What would Mr A-List do? He would quickly decide that Mr Big was clearly unnerved by his own particular A-List sparkle or he wouldn't be trying to be so BIG in the first place. Instead of feeling put down, simply invoke your inner A-Lister and take it all as a great compliment.

A friend of my partner's, who is a well-known movie actor, applied a similar idea brilliantly. He once confided that fans could sometimes be quite brusque and almost rude when meeting him. He knew that his fans would often be nervous so they might come across as rude because they felt awkward and tongue-tied. Knowing that their demeanour was saying lots about them rather than being about him, he certainly didn't take their surliness as an insult. Interestingly, he felt it was one of the biggest compliments they could give him. This focused way of thinking, firmly rooted in the good, has ensured his continued success as one of the most well-known faces in America... and totally A-List!

Most people, when they encounter someone new for the first time, share a tendency to 'mark themselves down' in comparison. All too often, we assume that new people are accomplished, knowledgeable and confident because they are an unknown quantity; our suburban zombie plays on that unknown quantity, and gets us to think the worst. 'They must be more accomplished than us, better go and mark ourselves down, then!' But if we are marking ourselves down in comparison to others, the likelihood is they are marking themselves down too! Once we realise this, we can really make progress in freeing ourselves from the grip of our doubting, limiting zombie. Don't mark yourself down, mark yourself up and share your fabulousness with the world.

Once you realise most people mark themselves down in any new encounter, then you can choose to mark yourself up instead. You can begin from an assumed position of accomplishment and strength. Channel your inner A-Lister, play and have fun, giving your best accomplished and polished performance. Here's an example of this in my life. I was with a group of friends and one of them had started dating someone much younger than us. Our friend had brought her new flame along and the new flame seemed bored, not in the least bit talkative, uncomfortable and keen to leave as early as possible. Each and every one of us assumed that our friend's new flame thought we were too old, boring and not cool enough. Some time later, after our friend and her younger partner had established a relationship, we learned the real reason for the initial coolness. The younger person had marked himself down, assuming we were more interesting, more intelligent and generally intimidating precisely because we were older. Lots of people are marking themselves down all the time, so don't join them. Mark yourself up and enjoy playing the game of life!

Another way to understand this concept is if we look at that classic worry of: 'What are the new neighbours going to be like???' How many times when our old neighbours move out do we feel anxious about the new arrivals on the block? Will they be awkward and difficult? Almost none of us puts ourselves in their shoes and imagines that they may be thinking the same about US!!!' If new people are nerve-wracking for you, then you are probably just as nerve-wracking for them. Think about it and mark yourself up!

In addition, if you apply the principle of the Law of Attraction, if you expect new people to be difficult, in all likelihood you will attract seeing that side of their character.

Imagine everyone you meet is a great potential friend and teacher with a gift to impart to you and you will have better experiences with new people. As that attitude becomes embedded in your belief system, you will bring more of those kinds of people with those attributes into your life.

Writing the script of your own life and making it fabulous

Lots of us watch television programmes and see the glamour and adventure of the characters on screen. We are gripped by what happens each week. We watch these shows from the safety of our sofas or armchairs and think that we can't have amazing and wonderful things ourselves because life is happening to us and we have no control over what comes into our experience. But the truth is that we are the authors of our own lives and we are writing the script of our day-to-day experiences all the time.

Let's explore this idea a little further. Let's imagine our lives as a television show running year on year. Sometimes it can feel as if we've been birthed into a dreary soap opera. It can feel as if great things will never come our way. We have become the victims of a belief pattern that says we can rarely transform our lives. But if we really regard life as a TV show, what's to stop us being the first person to leave for a brand new role in a more exciting, more fabulous show. You can choose to play a bit part in a kitchen sink drama all your life, or you can choose to walk away and become the A-List star of a glamorous soap. Which do you want?

There is a curious truth about human experience and the Universal Mind: you are not only the viewer of the television show of your life but you are the director and producer as well. So how's this season looking? Is it time for a rewrite? Is your show fabulous and top of the ratings or is it floundering? If it's floundering, then it's definitely time to change that unpopular and negative storyline and inject a little A-List sparkle.

How do you re-write that all-important script? You change your thoughts and your focus. This changes your emotions and you begin to feel great. You change the direction of travel of your life and the show you are watching week after week - the story of your life - will begin slowly but surely to play out a brand new storyline, one that you want to see.

To help you with evaluating your current life story, you can consider all the things that are currently happening in your life. Are there people who are totally dominated by their zombies and are consistently bringing you down with their own focus on limitation and lack? If so, do they need to be gradually squeezed out of your show until they are ex cast members who make the occasional guest appearance? Are there those A-Listers who make guest appearances currently who you want to make into full-time cast members?

Thinking of your life as the script of a show takes the emotional heat out of

114

observing your current situation. After all, if a TV show is flagging in the ratings what do the scriptwriters do? They change the storyline! You are the star and the viewer in your life show and you can change your storyline. I found it helped me to write my goals down and stick them up on the wall in front of my bed. Every night when I went to sleep, I saw them and every day when I woke up, I saw them again. One goal might be: 'I have interesting friends.' Another might be: 'I have exciting career opportunities.' If you focus on these things with a firm belief and move in the direction of your goals by meeting people or looking for jobs, then circumstances will change to bring these things to you. You have only to expect it and put it out there.

Bringing fabulous people and circumstances into your life

Another way of bringing better people and experiences into your life is to try the following tactic. I looked at all the people I knew. I wanted to have a focus on improving my experiences and having the best time. I googled the words 'Fabulous' and 'Abundance' and found a bright digital image of each word. I printed them out and put them on the bathroom mirror. I then printed photos of people I knew and liked and stuck them on my mirror under categories of 'Great People', 'Helpful People' and 'Stellar People'. Finally, underneath the words and pictures I printed in big bold letters: 'More Please. Thank you!' What happened over the next few months was amazing. I found my time was increasingly taken up with meeting all the great, helpful and stellar people I liked. The helpful people did things that were of huge benefit such as supporting at a launch event or helping me with my career development. I also learned wonderful life lessons from the stellar people. And the other amazing thing was that the people I didn't really like spending time with - those potential ex cast members - began to call or email less and less until eventually they melted away altogether.

You can look at situations in your life and ask yourself the question: 'Is what I am doing here part of having a fabulous and abundant life? If the answer is no then why am I doing it? What can I do instead to up my fabulousness quotient?' That can be something as simple as saving up to go out for a REALLY GLAM night or stay at a REALLY GLAM hotel. If you do this regularly the Universe will begin to bring circumstances into your life that will enable you to have more glamorous experiences. It cannot tell whether what you are doing is the current truth of your life or not, so it will act to bring your life into line and to make it true for you. If you want to stay at the Ritz but can't afford it, go there and have a coffee and stay for two hours. Doing so, you become the kind of person who spends time at the Ritz. This becomes true for you. But if you never even show up at the Ritz, it can never become true for you.

When I first moved back to London, I was recently divorced and at the grand old age of forty-three, I was living back at my father's house. To make matters worse, my bedroom at my dad's was decorated with children's jungle wallpaper. As I lay in bed at night staring up at the lions and tigers on the wall, my suburban zombie tried to tell me that this was what I had ultimately been reduced to. I had had a go at life and should be glad that I hadn't lost everything and wasn't living in a bedsit. 'You're washed up,' said zombie. 'As far as relationships go, everyone wants a twenty one year-old, no-one will be remotely interested in you.' Fortunately I was having none of that rubbish in my ear. My A-List me took my zombie down. The A-List me was grateful for the lesson from this that there was only one way I could now go... and that was UP! I stripped the wallpaper, whitewashed the walls and began internet dating. I was looking to meet more friends and hopefully that special someone. I wanted to meet vibrant and interesting people and to have a bit more glamour in my life to boot!

I began dating but I immediately realised that many of the men on dating websites were looking for something other than a long-term relationship. Some were already in a relationship and using internet dating to cheat on their partner, others lied about jobs or their appearance, using ten year old photos of themselves on their profile, and all sorts of other unhelpful shenanigans. I decided to begin looking at other dating avenues and found a bespoke introduction agency where I had a dating consultant who would tailor the dates to my needs. This was not cheap and I could have easily walked away, but instead I figured that if other men were prepared to pay the same amount of money then they would be serious about finding a relationship. Plus, I was worth it and having some glamorous and fabulous nights out would bring more of the same into my life regardless of what my income was now.

I dipped into my savings and paid for six months' membership. Although I didn't meet a long-term partner, I did go out to lovely restaurants with interesting and very genuine guys and I did dress up to the nines and look and feel fabulous while doing it. Even more importantly I was meeting men who were serious about finding a partner, every single one of them, down to the last man! Even though I didn't meet anyone as a partner for me, the Universe continued by the Law of Attraction to bring me more and more opportunities to meet men who were serious about finding someone. Consequently, I signed up to a very reputable dating website (recommended by a friend I had made through the bespoke dating agency). Eight months later I had met the love of my life. He is intelligent, loving, kind, thoughtful, generous of spirit and cute as a button! We go out to lots of high end A-List restaurants every week and have an amazing life together.

The main thing to remember here is that if you think and expect things to change in a certain way in your life and you make your direction of travel move towards that change even in the smallest of ways, the Law of Attraction will make it happen. It has no choice! It's inevitable.

So, look at the TV show of your life. Prepare to rewrite that script. Make your show glam rather than kitchen sink. Fill it with great, helpful and stellar cast members with the star of the show being the one and only... YOU!

Playing the part and loving the selfie!

Life is serious fun, so treat it that way. Be serious about having fun and PLAY. Live it up, laugh it up and love it up. If life is a game, then we need to play to have maximum fun.

If we want to have a fabulous life, then it is very important to be serious about that fun factor. Think of every event as a game and have fun with your role in it. Think about what kind of person you want to be and then make a firm affirmation: 'I am this kind of person so this is how I am going to present myself to the world.' It might be that you want to be a natty dresser, or a more spiritual being in tune with your inner peace, or any number of things. So decide which role you are going to play in the game of life and present yourself to the world in that way. How you present yourself to the world signals, in turn, the kind of game you want to play. You can play a game where you are the underdog, the shy retiring loser in life, or you can play the role where you are the fabulous A-Lister who succeeds in the game, bringing more and more abundance into your life by focusing on exactly that.

You will be surprised how quickly the rest of the world will fall into supporting this view of yourself and how increasingly that persona will become your reality. The Universe won't argue with you. If you say 'Yes I am', the Universe will say 'Yes you are.' It's inevitable. You have only to make a contract with yourself to believe in the part you want to play, and give it all you've got. If you have no faith in it, then the persona will quickly fall away before it has even got off the ground. It's okay to slip up and lose your focus occasionally - we all do that as human beings - but in the main you should be playing the part of the new improved you the majority of the time. That is what will eventually make it commonplace and part of your reality through the Universal Law. Eventually you won't be playing any more, it will have become your truth. After all, children dress up and play a part during their games with each other all the time. They love taking on different personas and trying them out for size. When did we grown-ups become so boring and stop doing that? It sounds like the best fun EVER!

You can reinforce and embed this fabulously abundant A-List you by making good use of that wonderful smart phone invention, the selfie. Take pictures of yourself when you are out at great places, feeling great, looking great, and having a fabulous time. Take pictures of the venues: from cool cafes to that glitzy restaurant you saved up for. Put all these photos in a folder on your phone and look at them often saying to yourself: 'This is my abundant life. This is the fabulous me. I am the A-Lister. This is who I am.'

You can even surround yourself with pictures of people you don't know, or places you haven't been, that reflect that new dazzling you. So if you want to be more cool and trendy, collect pictures from the internet of people or places that embody that. Save them on your smart phone and look at them regularly. The Universe will ensure that, increasingly, you will be surrounded by people who are cool and trendy who can advise you, for instance, on what to buy to look your best. Or you will be drawn to things that will offer you what you want - an affordable boutique with great clothes and a friendly shop assistant who knows his or her stuff and will help you choose your new look.

Let's explore how this works a little further. Suppose you come across a new word you haven't seen or heard before; suddenly you notice that word everywhere around you - on billboards, in magazines, adverts and conversations. The Universal Law of Attraction works by the same principle. The things we want are already there in the reality surrounding us - focusing on them brings them forth more clearly and sharply, so we can grasp them. They become our truth.

When I met my partner, we started going out to art gallery private viewings and to A-list functions. I had started to feel bolder in those situations but it was no mean feat and it still felt like a bit of an uncomfortable struggle. The suburban zombie's little voice in my head started saying: 'Oh no, you just aren't ready for all this. You'll never make it. You're not like these people, they have a certain glamour and artistic coolness. They are the ones with the artistic licence, not you. You're just some guy who works on rights and well-being.' Then I thought about the idea of playing a part. I looked at my full name and decided that today I would play the part of the fabulous, cool and fascinating Will J. Jackson. This immediately took me out of myself and that freed version of me was able to say: 'The whole world is working for me! It's all a game so let's play it. How is this situation a game?'

I put on my most interesting clothes, often with something eye-catching and unusual to get me noticed. I expected people to look and marvel at my fabulousness. I looked that way and I walked that way and it wasn't long before I talked that way too! Don't forget that many people are a slave to their suburban zombies. They are far too busy worrying about whether they come across as good enough themselves to spend energy undermining you. If you act the part of the one who is different and fabulous and really believe it, by the Law of Attraction, the people who find you to be so will be increasingly drawn into your path. Play it out and it will become a firm reality for you. So now it wasn't my everyday me, victim of that incredibly destructive inner suburban zombie, who was in control. It was the ultra-special A-List me who was taking over the reins. Within weeks, I was breezing into the snazziest, hippest, most outrageous celebrity-strewn arty party with my head held high and dressed up to the nines! I wasn't the person who looked and felt inadequate glancing nervously around at others. I was the one who was looked at by others and it felt GREAT!

You can channel and you can be that A-Lister! Your own personal beauty and interestingness lies in any area. It can be your quirky way of laughing or your geeky interest in sci-fi. We're not talking about physical beauty here. Beauty comes in every shape and form. Don't buy into the nonsense that you are only beautiful if you are good looking. After all, there are movie stars who are great looking and others who aren't, but they are all still movie stars with interesting and attractive qualities we love and want to see. You really don't have to conform to the ideals of what is physically gorgeous to be captivating and stunning. Don't buy into that load of baloney! What are the great things on your own personal Fab-o-meter? Make a list of the qualities that you feel are good about you. Look at them daily on your phone and focus on them to embed them as your internal and external truth.

It doesn't matter what changes you're looking for in life. It doesn't matter how much you want to 'up' the rating on your personal Fab-o-meter of life. All you have to do is put your belief in the new you and act that part as much as you can. It might be tricky at first. I know this from personal experience. But it will embed the more you do it with faith and conviction. And if anybody, however well intentioned, throws you one of those niggling negative comments about the way you are changing, just remember to raise those shields because you don't want that rubbish in your ear!! They just want you to surrender to the same little suburban zombie who has enslaved them and why on earth would you want to do that? Build and embed your own truth... not theirs! You're on life's A-List and abundance constantly flows your way, and don't you forget it!

If you are having trouble being positive about yourself, here is a useful little method you can try which worked very well for me. First we'll return to that idea of your life as a television show in which you have the leading role. Now ask the question: 'If I wanted to convince an actor to play me in the TV show of my life, what great qualities would I say my character has?' You can expand this idea by asking yourself this question: 'If someone was going to be me, and live my life for a week, what good things about my life would I tell them to persuade them to do it?' Write down what you would say and then SAY IT and record it on the voice memo in your smart phone. Play it back to yourself on your way to work, on your way home, standing in a queue... wherever. Play it, believe it and it will increasingly become who you are and what your life is.

So remember, if you believe that life is a game, you'll be amazed at how much of a game it really is. Play it and have fun! Focus on the A-List you - that person is you... if you believe it and you keep at it. It's inevitable!

PART THREE: Top tips

Unleashing your inner A-Lister

i.   Don't beat yourself up when your zombie rises up on any occasion. Everyone is vulnerable to a zombie attack from time to time. Just take it as a lesson learned and re-focus on the fabulous A-List you.

ii.   Regular check-ins with your Fabulous Abundance Buddy can help boost each other's A-List potential. Set regular times to meet in person, by phone, FaceTime, Skype or email.

iii. Compliments are a gift that people have had the thoughtfulness to give you - and it is rude to refuse a gift. Accept compliments with a firm 'Thank you.' And an internal: 'Yes I am!'

iv.   When people say good things about you, record them on your phone and look at them regularly. This will lift your self-image, your mood and therefore the

people and experiences that you attract
to you in the course of your day.

v.   Make your decisions based on unlimited
     abundance instead of fear and lack.

vi. The majority of us are marking ourselves
     down in comparison with other people.
     If you realise that others are marking
     themselves down just as much as you
     are, you can begin to mark yourself up,
     and give the gift of the wonderful
     fabulousness of you to the world.

vii. See everyone you meet as a wonderful
     friend and teacher with a gift to impart,
     and that is precisely what you will attract
     into your life: both wonderful friends
     and teachers.

viii. We are all the authors of our lives and
      we are writing the script of our day-to-
      day experiences all the time. So change
      those negative storylines and inject a
      little A-List sparkle into the script of

your future by changing your thoughts and focus.

ix. Write your goals down and stick them up on the wall in front of your bed. Every night when you go to sleep and every day when you wake up, they will be what you see. This will powerfully bring those things into your future.

x. Create your own fabulous abundance wall with the people you want in your life who are great, helpful and stellar. The Universal Law of Attraction will bring more of these people into your life and less of those people you don't want.

xi. Spend time at great places often and the Law of Attraction will increasingly make it easier for you to be at those wonderful places in the future.

xii. Think and expect things to change in a certain way in your life. Move towards that change, even in the smallest ways, and the Law of Attraction with make it happen. Because that is its function – to attract what you focus on.

xiii. Life is a game so play it and have fun! How you present yourself to the world signals the kind of game you want to play. Focusing on fabulous abundance means you are playing the A-List you who will increasingly attract more and more abundance and success into your day-to-day life.

xiv. The Universe won't argue with you. If you say 'Yes I am fabulous and my life is abundant', the Universe will say 'Yes you are and yes it is.' It's inevitable.

xv. Develop and embed the fabulous A-List factor in your life by taking selfies when you are out at great places, feeling great, looking great, and having a fabulous time. Put these in a folder on your phone and look at them often affirming to yourself: 'This is who I am!'

xvi. Collect pictures from the internet of the kinds of people you want to get to know or the places you want to frequent. Again, keep them in a file on your phone and look at them often. The universe will bring these kinds of people and places to you.

xvii. Ask yourself: 'If I wanted to convince an actor to play me in the TV show of my life, what great qualities would I say my character has?' Or: 'If someone was going to be me, and live my life for a week, what good things about my life would I tell them to persuade them to do it?' Record your responses on the voice memo on your phone. Play it back to yourself on your way to work, waiting for a friend, whenever and wherever. The more you listen, the more it will become who you are and what your life is.

The final word

The final word

In conclusion, the following points form a final summary of the top tips from this book:

i.   The Law of Attraction is a natural law like the law of gravity and, as such, is acting in all our lives, all the time.

ii.   Applying right thinking to bring positive change into your life through the Law of Attraction can take time. It is not a quick fix, so be patient. Some changes can take hours, others days, weeks or months; and others can take years. But keep focused and know that the change you want WILL come.

iii. Everyone is a teacher and can impart gifts to you about living a better life, just as you are a great teacher for others. Even difficult people are teaching you something worthwhile so always ask of every person and situation: 'What is the gift here?'

iv. Uplifting music to start your day can put you on that positive plane and attract positive experiences into your life hour by hour.

v. Your Fabulous Abundance Buddy can help you explore how you are engaging with the fundamental principles of the Law of Attraction and share good ideas, experiences and ways forward. Have you found your buddy and booked your first check-in?

vi. Your inner suburban zombie will try to hold you back with limiting beliefs and small-minded ideas. Realise when this is happening and take your zombie down! There's a fantastic accomplished version of you just waiting to get out...

vii. Compliments are a gift and it's rude to refuse a gift. Accept them with a firm 'Yes I am!'

viii. When people give you compliments note them down in your phone under 'How others see me.' Whenever your inner zombie tells you that you are not good enough, you'll have hard evidence that the truth is really very different!

ix.   Great statements saved as wallpapers on your smart phone can give you a welcome right-thinking boost. Looking at your phone, while standing in a queue or waiting for someone, will help you to focus on those positive statements and the more you focus on them, the more they become true for you. This has to be so through the Universal Law of Attraction.

x.   When people start talking in negative ways about how bad life is, don't buy into that unless you want it to be your reality too. Whenever this happens just say inside your head: 'Raise shields! That is not the truth!' Or something that works for you to block out the tidal wave of negativity promulgated by others.

xi. Make a vow, now, to base your decisions
     in the firm knowledge of your fantastic
     future and make fewer and fewer
     decisions based in fear and limitation.

xii. Many of us have a tendency to mark
     ourselves down in all sorts of situations.
     Nobody is more special than anyone else
     and others are probably marking
     themselves down in comparison to you,
     so always mark yourself up and have a
     great time!

xiii. If the Law of Attraction is working for all
     of us all the time, then if someone does
     something wrong to you, they are
     putting out a negative energy into the
     Universe and it will come back to them
     even if you aren't there to see it first-
     hand. Use this concept consciously to
     avoid getting wound up by the actions
     and attitudes of others. Comeuppance
     must come, but don't revel in this as that
     is putting negativity out there that will
     come back on you.

xiv. You can't change anybody else. Only they can change and it has to come from inside because they want to. However, you can literally 'get on the good side' of a person by focusing on the good things about them.

xv. Only ever go on hard evidence in the judgements you make about people and situations. As creatures raised on a diet of negativity, we humans often choose to make a negative assumption if we choose to make any assumption at all. Stop yourself and ask: 'Where's my real evidence for thinking this?' Quite often there isn't any, it's just plain old negative thinking again.

xvi. You are the author of your own life show and you are writing the script of your future episodes. Change your thoughts to focus on fabulous abundance and change your life show from kitchen sink drama to glam soap where you are the central character and everything is going your way!

xvii. Write your goals down and stick them up on the wall in front of your bed. Every time you go to sleep you will see them as well as every time you wake up. This will embed your positive personal mind-set.

xviii. Bring better people and experiences into your life by sticking the words 'Fabulous Abundance' on your bathroom mirror as well as pictures of people who are great, helpful and stellar... at the bottom write MORE PLEASE!

xix. Don't just change your thoughts, but make your direction of travel the same as those thoughts. The more you think and act as if it is true, the more the Universe will bring it to you in order to make it true for you.

xx. This is not just about positive thinking and soldiering through in the face of adversity... it's about positive knowing. It's that firm and unyielding expectation that underpins everything and brings about change for the good.

xxi. You don't have to conform to the ideal of what is physically gorgeous to be captivating and stunning. Don't buy into that load of baloney! What are the great things on your own personal Fab-o-meter? Make a list of the qualities that you feel are good about you. Look at them daily in your phone or on a piece of notepaper.

xxii. If you wanted to convince an actor to play you in the TV show of your life, what great qualities would you say your character has? If you wanted to expand this idea to consider the positive aspects in your life as a whole, then you could also ask yourself this question: 'If someone was going to be you and live your life for a week, what good things about your life would you tell them to persuade them to do it?'

xxiii. If you want to have a fabulous life then it is very important to be serious about the fun factor. Life is serious fun, so treat it that way. Be serious about having fun and PLAY. Live it up, laugh it up and love it up.

Will J. Jackson

Will J. Jackson has been developing approaches to New Thought ideas since 2009. He has encouraged individuals to see the limitless potential available to them through their application of the principles of the Law of Attraction.

As an education adviser he has specialised in strategies to promote well-being. During his time as an adviser for The United Nations Children's Fund he has worked on a programme to raise young people's self esteem and aspirations through equitable rights based approaches to daily living. The impact of this work has been to empower young people to gain a greater sense of self worth through an understanding of the interconnectedness they share with others.

With *The Zombie of Suburbia* Will J. Jackson brings the distillation/practical application of this knowledge and experience to millions.

www.willjackson.guru

Made in the USA
Charleston, SC
12 September 2015